EDGE BOOKS

DARING FLOOD RESCUES

D0317313

AMY WAESCHLE

Consultant:
Jackie White, Captain of Fire Investigations
and Homeland Security, Albuquerque Fire Department

527 325 56 4

Raintree is an imprint of Capstone Global Library Limited, a company incorporated in England and Wales having its registered office at 264 Banbury Road, Oxford, OX2 7DY – Registered company number: 6695582

www.raintree.co.uk
myorders@raintree.co.uk

Edited by Lauren Dupuis-Perez
Designed by Sara Radka
Production by Katy LaVigne
Printed and bound in India

ISBN 978 1 4747 5390 6
22 21 20 19 18
10 9 8 7 6 5 4 3 2 1

British Library Cataloguing in Publication Data
A full catalogue record for this book is available from the British Library.

Quote Sources
p.8, "From Festivities to Flood Waters." Royal National Lifeboat Institution, 7 March 2016; p.11, "Cyclone Debbie: SES Rescuers Just Minutes from Being Swept Away." *The Australian*, 3 April 2017; p.16, "First Responders Save Trapped Airmen During Typhoon Neoguri." U.S. Air Force, 17 July 2014; p.21, "Woman, Baby Rescued by Coast Guard from Flooding." WCJL Savannah, 21 July 2017; p.24, "Toowoomba's 'Miracle Girl' Surfaces After Being Feared Drowned." *The Australian*, 20 January 2011; p.28, "A Night of Faith and Courage." *The Tillamook Headlight Herald*, 8 November 2008

Acknowledgements
Getty Images: Ben Pruchnie, 8, Colin Anderson, Cover, Dan Proud Photography, 22, bottom 24, David McNew, 28, gdagys, 26, H20addict, Cover, Handout, 15, Jason O'Brien, 10, 11, Jeff J Mitchell, middle 17, 29, Mark Kolbe, 12, 13, bottom 17, Michael Nagle, top 17, Paul Frederiksen, Jr., 27, Sean Rayford, 19, 21, 25; iStockphoto: kyrien, 4; Newscom: Kyodo, 14, Owen Humphreys/PA Wire/ZUMAPRESS, 9, Peter Byrne/PA Wire/ZUMAPRESS, 6, Splash, top 24, Yonhap News/YNA, 16; Wikimedia: Flickr, 23, Petty Officer 3rd Class Jon-Paul Rios, 18, U.S. Air Force photo by Tech. Sgt. Parker Gyokeres, 20

Graphic elements by Capstone Press and Book Buddy Media.

Rescues in floods

A single flood can cost a country billions of pounds in damages as buildings, cars, roads and bridges are destroyed.

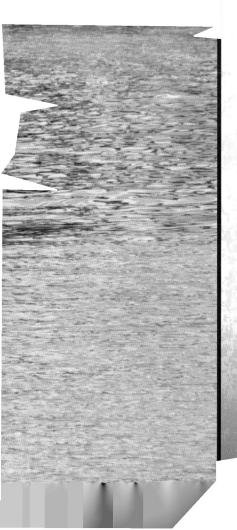

It has been raining for days and the rivers are swollen with water. Rain continues to pour down. In one river, a dam breaks. The water rushes onto the land. It's a flood!

Floods can occur in several ways. Rivers or creeks can burst their banks. A storm or **tsunami** can wash the sea onto the land. Too much rain can cause **drainage** systems to become overburdened. Floods are the second-most deadly natural disasters, after wildfires. Thousands of people around the world die each year from floods. Moving water can destroy houses, uproot trees and carry off cars.

Most floods happen slowly, developing over hours or sometimes days. This gives people time to prepare their homes for the floodwaters or to **evacuate**.

Some floods happen quickly, with no warning. People can get trapped. In these situations, they need to be rescued. Rescuers must brave the rising waters to come to their aid. Read on to discover true stories of daring rescues amidst the chaos of floods.

tsunami large, destructive wave caused by an underwater earthquake or volcano

drainage way to get rid of extra water

evacuate leave a dangerous place to go somewhere safer

On 6 December 2015, north of England, it had been raining hard for two days. Storm Desmond whipped the wind up to gusts of 130 kilometres (80 miles) per hour. The storm had dumped more than 33 centimetres (13 inches) of rain. Kevin and Mary Holmes were taking care of their grandsons, Sebastian and Jacob, in Cumbria, as the storm raged. A cousin and his girlfriend were also visiting. Over a couple of hours, nearby rivers burst their banks. The water moving past their home was too fast for them to escape. They were trapped. Then the water started seeping into the house.

Kevin called for help. His grandsons climbed into the top bunk of their bed. Kevin and Mary used torches to signal for help in the dark night. The water in the house continued to rise. There was nowhere to go.

Emergency workers helped evacuate thousands of people after Storm Desmond flooded parts of the United Kingdom in 2015.

How to survive a flood

Most of the time, floods happen slowly. Listen to the radio or TV reports during storms. These will let you know if you need to evacuate. If you need to leave, keep these things in mind:

- Move quickly to higher ground, but do not walk through floodwaters. Even a few centimetres of moving water can knock you down.

- Cars caught in just 30 cm (1 foot) of moving water can be swept away. If you are in a car but the water is not moving, get out and move to higher ground. If the water is moving, stay inside the car and signal for help.

Volunteers from the Royal National Lifeboat Institution (RNLI) hurried to the scene. But the water surrounding the house was moving swiftly, and it was too shallow for a boat. Luckily, a farmer driving a tractor asked if he could help. Two RNLI volunteers hopped into the tractor. The farmer took them across the floodwaters. While the volunteers reassured the family, the farmer returned for the rest of the rescuers, who had inflated a raft.

With the raft tied onto the tractor, the farmer returned to the house. The waters inside had risen about another 30 cm (1 foot). Rescuers loaded the family members into the raft, two at a time, and the farmer towed them to safety. Once they evacuated the entire family, the rescuers took them to a local pub to warm up.

> **"I am indebted to the RNLI – not only for putting their lives at risk to rescue my family, but for being awesome human beings."**
>
> **HELEN HOLMES**
> MOTHER OF
> SEBASTIAN AND JACOB

Rescue workers carry poles when surveying an area. They use the poles to check the water depth.

In 2015 rescue teams rafted people through the flooded streets of Carlisle in Cumbria (above). One year after Storm Desmond, the water had cleared, but some damage still remained (below).

CHAPTER 2

House swept away

Cyclone Debbie caused the deaths of six people in northeast Australia.

Flooded roads can trap people in their homes.

WATER
STOP OVER
ROAD

Cyclone Debbie was dumping rain on New South Wales, Australia, on 2 April 2017. The Albert River was flooded. The town of Luscombe was filled with water. Helen Gallo's house flooded quickly. Gallo, her two children and their grandfather climbed onto the roof of their garage as floodwaters rose steadily.

Gallo called the police for help 16 times. But police told her that rescuers could not reach her house. Gallo and her two children waited in the dark for four hours, hoping for a rescue. Then the garage roof started to sink beneath Gallo's feet. Her children helped pull her up onto the roof of the main house.

> **"**All of the sudden, I've turned around and the garage started sinking. It's fallen underneath me and these two little ones have just grabbed my arms and I had to pull myself back up.**"**
>
> **HELEN GALLO**

cyclone hurricane that occurs in the southwestern Pacific or Indian Oceans

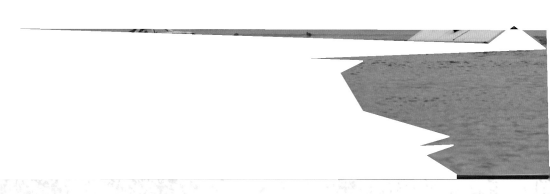

It took emergency service rescuers another hour to reach the house, which was surrounded by floodwaters. The team included Claire Browning, a nurse, Chris Holloway, a medical worker, and team leader Jim Ferguson. Their way was blocked by downed power lines, trees and fences. The team of three finally arrived. They tied their rescue boat to the house.

Ferguson climbed up the side of the house to reach the family. The family and the grandfather's two dogs were helped into the boat. Rescuers whisked them all to dry land. Minutes later, they heard the house break away from its foundations. It floated downstream and smashed into another house. Minutes later, it hit several trees and broke apart completely.

Swiftwater rescuers

Water moving at 19 km (12 miles) per hour has the same force as more than 230 kilograms (500 pounds). Rescuers can be swept up by moving water. For safety, swiftwater rescue crews follow the rule "reach, throw, row and go".

- **Reach**: Swiftwater rescuers first try to reach the victim. They use a long-handled tool that the victim can grab.

- **Throw**: If that doesn't work, rescuers will throw a rope. They use this rope to tow the victim to shore.

- **Row**: If a rope fails rescue crews will try to launch a boat.

- **Go**: Only if there is no other option will rescuers swim to the victim.

CHAPTER 3
Typhoon floods Japan

Typhoon Neoguri brought heavy rains, which caused massive flooding and deadly landslides in parts of Japan.

Scientists track major storms, such as Typhoon Neoguri, with satellite photos.

On 9 July 2014, two United States Air Force airmen, Brandon Miles and Roderick Jones, had been awake all night. **Typhoon** Neoguri had hit Kadena, Japan. Rain had been falling non-stop on the US Air Force base there. Miles and Jones were on duty in a guardhouse. By dawn, there were several centimetres of water on the ground surrounding the guardhouse. But Jones and Miles weren't worried. The water didn't look dangerous.

Around 6.30 a.m., they heard a crash, like waves slamming against a ship. It was a flood. Brown water loaded with **debris** rushed past the guardhouse. The airmen tried to open the door, but it wouldn't budge. They were trapped.

Miles and Jones radioed for help. But rescue patrols were busy helping residents. Finally, a crew of security personnel was organized. They raced to the scene. One of the base's fire trucks also came. They had to break through several gates to reach the guardhouse. By the time they arrived, the guardhouse was almost **submerged**.

typhoon hurricane that forms in the western Pacific Ocean

debris pieces that are left after something has been destroyed

submerged under water

Inside the shack, water had almost filled the space. Miles and Jones were treading water. Their heads were up against the ceiling. They had only centimetres of room left to breathe. Rescuers tried to break through the roof with an electric saw, but the saw broke. So they took turns trying to break through using axes and sledgehammers. Finally a firefighter arrived with a new saw blade. Within minutes, they cut a hole in the roof and pulled the airmen out.

"I looked into the hole and saw no more than fifteen to twenty cm (six to eight inches) of breathing space left. The lives of these two airmen were in our hands. It's only that we had faith in each other and confidence in one another that this rescue operation was a success."

MASTER SERGEANT AARON DUGGINS
RESCUER

Typhoon Neoguri pushed waves to heights of 12 metres (40 feet).

Flood rescue tools

Flood responders might be volunteers, members of the military or police. They all carry special equipment to get the job done.

Boat or raft: In calm water, rescuers can "float" victims through flooded streets. They use inflatable boats, kayaks or canoes. Sometimes they use household items, such as a refrigerator door! In swift water, rescuers may use motor boats.

Tools: Rescue crews may need to use electric saws, bolt cutters, crowbars or axes to free victims trapped by rising water.

Safety gear: Rescuers wear helmets, life jackets and wetsuits or drysuits. These suits help keep them warm when floodwaters are cold.

CHAPTER 4

Coast Guard to the rescue

Highly trained members of the US Coast Guard often use helicopters for flood rescues. With a helicopter, rescuers can respond quickly to places that are too dangerous to reach by car or lorry.

Rain fell for days in South Carolina, USA. By 5 October 2015, the amount of rain had set records. Many cities were experiencing flooding, including Charleston, the largest city in the state. Rivers and creeks overflowed, and dams broke under the strain.

Cristi Mueller and her family were aware of the flooding, but thought they would be safe. There were no warnings or evacuation orders for their area. But floodwaters kept rising. Water came into the house. Mueller escaped with her baby girl to a neighbour's roof. Mueller tried to get help by calling the emergency services. When that didn't work, she called the Coast Guard.

In times of emergency, rescue teams search for stranded people.

All US Coast Guard rescue helicopters have a stainless-steel rescue basket on board.

Because the flooding in the area was so severe, there were no local rescue vehicles available. Coast Guard helicopter pilots Jeffrey Tucker and Derek Lehr and their team were at their station in Savannah, Georgia, more than 130 km (80 miles) away. As soon as they got Mueller's call, they suited up and took off in their MH-65 Dolphin rescue helicopter. The flight was several hours long. Intense rain made the flight difficult. When they arrived, the pilots found a flooded neighborhood. Debris was drifting around the houses and cars were underwater. Mueller's home was almost completely submerged.

Rescue swimmer Jack Lacey was lowered to the roof with a basket. He loaded Mueller and her baby into it. But there were no straps to keep them in. Mueller had to cling to her baby for dear life as they were raised up and into the helicopter. She rode in the open helicopter to a nearby airport. Shortly after, Mueller's husband and their son were rescued by boat.

"I was extremely nervous, probably the most terrifying moment of my life . . . holding onto your fifteen-month-old daughter just that far up was incredibly frightening, but we made it. We closed our eyes, we prayed and everyone was wonderful."

CRISTI MUELLER

Rescue teams may use inflatable motor boats to reach people trapped in floods.

Flash flood in Queensland

The flash flood that hit the Toowoomba area in 2011 claimed the lives of about 20 people.

In the flash flood that hit the areas of Toowoomba and Grantham in 2011, first responders from local police and fire departments saved many people.

By the beginning of 2011, eastern Australia had experienced months of extra-heavy **seasonal** rains. Many rivers were at their highest levels. Some had flooded. Crops were ruined and coal mines had filled with water. A cyclone made flooding worse by dumping another 25 cm (10 inches) of rain. Many towns were submerged or **isolated** by flooding rivers.

On 10 January in the town of Toowoomba, a thunderstorm caused a **flash flood**. The car that Hannah Reardon-Smith and her mother, Katherine, were in was swept away. The wall of brown water smashed their car into a telephone pole. The current pinned them there. They climbed onto the car's roof. Other cars and debris raced past. Bystanders watched from a parking garage, unable to help.

seasonal happening during a particular time of the year

isolated all alone

flash flood a flood that happens with little or no warning, often during periods of heavy rainfall

News reports called Hannah Reardon-Smith the "miracle girl". In this photo, Hannah (circled in white) is moments from being rescued.

Firefighter Peter McCarron answered the call to help. He waded out into the raging flood with his rescue gear. McCarron almost had Katherine secured to a rescue line, which he had attached to the telephone pole. Then a car floating by crashed into the Reardon-Smiths' car and freed it. Hannah fell into the water, and McCarron lost his grip on Katherine. Both mother and daughter were swept away.

Luckily, other rescuers were downstream. One managed to pluck Hannah from the river. Katherine grabbed a stop sign. A bystander, Steven Seefeld, was able to reach her and pull her to safety. For his efforts, McCarron was awarded a silver medal for bravery. Both victims made a full recovery.

> "Hannah Reardon-Smith had no energy left. Another three seconds and she would have been dead."
>
> **STEVEN SEEFELD**

QUEENSLAND FIRE & RESCUE

In 2015 heavy rain fell for days in South Carolina, USA. It caused flash floods powerful enough to destroy entire roads.

Flash floods

Flash floods happen quickly. They often start in a canyon or narrow valley. Heavy rain falls over a short period of time, often in six hours or fewer. The ground becomes **saturated** with water. When the ground cannot hold any more, the water flows out all at once. It then rushes down the canyon or valley.

Flash floods are powerful. They can uproot trees, destroy houses and rip bridges off their foundations. Sometimes the only warning of an approaching flash flood is the roar of the rushing water. The best way to stay safe in a flash flood is to rush to higher ground.

saturated completely filled with something

CHAPTER 6

When the road ends

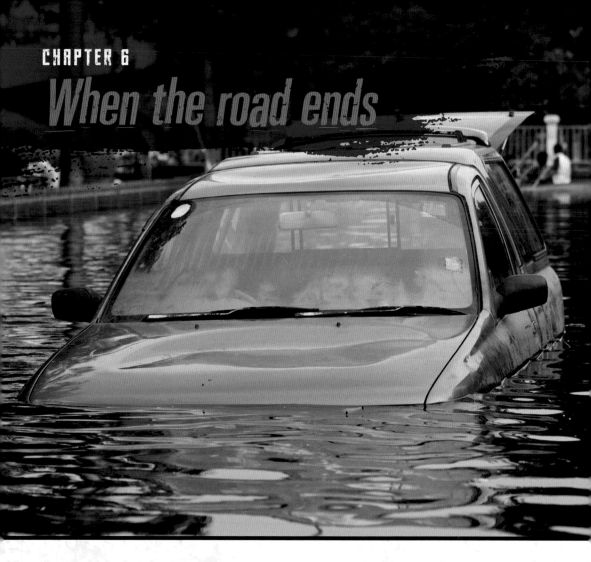

On 12 November 2008, Stephanie McRae was driving her three children home outside the town of Tillamook in Oregon, USA. A storm had hammered the area with rain all day. The rivers had become swift and swollen. Suddenly, McRae rounded a corner to see that the road had been washed away. She skidded into the hole. The car tumbled upside down into a creek, which had become a river 30 m (100 feet) wide. The car rolled upright and lodged against a **logjam**. The windows blew out and the car began filling with water.

logjam situation in which a large number of logs floating down a river become tangled with one another so that further movement is not possible

Being in your car can be very dangerous during a flood. If waters are rising it is important to avoid driving.

Eleven-year-old Maddie was in the front seat. Quickly, she scrambled out the back window and onto the roof. She called to her mother to pass her two siblings out to her. Stephanie did so and then followed. The four of them huddled on the roof of the car as the waters continued to rise. Maddie decided to go for help. She found a tree branch and crawled across it to the shore. Then she ran to a farmhouse and called the emergency services.

When the rescue team arrived, the water was up to Stephanie's waist. The captain decided to lower a 11-m (35-foot) ladder from one of their trucks. But it was still hanging 3 m (10 feet) above the three victims. The captain ordered firefighter Aaron Burris to crawl down the ladder. He was able to hoist each child and then their mother to safety.

> "If we'd rescued [Stephanie] a minute later, she'd be done. Tragedy was a heartbeat away. Everybody knew that. Call it luck, call it a miracle, but man, everything was working!"

SHERIFF'S OFFICE MARINE DEPUTY CHUCK REEDER
RESCUER

Many rescue workers use ladders to reach people caught in dangerous situations.

During floods, emergency workers are always looking and listening for people in need of rescue.

Floods can be deadly natural disasters, but flood rescue crews are hard at work around the world. When the waters begin to rise, these daring men and women are at work, saving lives.

Glossary

cyclone hurricane that occurs in the southwestern Pacific or Indian Oceans

debris pieces that are left after something has been destroyed

drainage way to get rid of extra water

evacuate leave a dangerous place to go somewhere safer

flash flood flood that happens with little or no warning, often during periods of heavy rainfall

isolated all alone

logjam situation in which a large number of logs floating down a river become tangled with one another so that further movement is not possible

saturated completely filled with something

seasonal happening during a particular time of the year

submerged under water

tsunami large, destructive wave caused by an underwater earthquake or volcano

typhoon hurricane that forms in the western Pacific Ocean

Find out more

Books

Extreme Fires and Floods (When Nature Attacks), John Farndon (Hungry Tomato, 2017)

Fierce Floods (Planet in Peril), Cath Senker (Wayland, 2017)

Floods (Nature Unleashed), Louise and Richard Spilsbury (Franklin Watts, 2017)

The World's Worst Floods (World's Worst Natural Disasters), John R Baker (Capstone, 2016)

Websites

**http://www.metoffice.gov.uk/guide/weather/
severe-weather-advice/flooding**
Learn about how to prepare for a flood and how to stay safe during and after a flood.

https://rnli.org/what-we-do/flood-rescue
Find out how the Royal National Lifeboat Institution manages search and rescue operations.

**https://www.natgeokids.com/uk/discover/geography/
physical-geography/causes-of-floods/**
Learn about what causes flooding around the world.

http://www.bbc.co.uk/guides/zcdqxsg
Read about the causes of flooding in the UK.

Index